Being Born

The Doula's Role

Being Born
The Doula's Role

Jewel Hernandez

Illustrations by
R. Michael Mithuna

HOHM PRESS
Prescott, Arizona

To Lee and the vision he holds, and to all the mothers & babies whose birthings taught me so much.

Special Thanks for all the support and learning from Ann Fulcher and the *Hearts and Hands* volunteer doulas, *Birth Resource Network* doulas, Gerri, Marla, Michelle and the San Diego midwives; and to Gerri, Nicole, Barb and Dani for help with photos.

Cover design, Layout and Interior Design: Zachary Parker, Kadak Graphics (www.kadakgraphics.com)
Cover and Interior Illustrations by R. Michael Mithuna

Library of Congress Cataloging-in-Publication Data:

Hernandez, Jewel.
 Being born : the doula's role / by Jewel Hernandez; illustrations by R. Michael Mithuna.
    p. cm.
 ISBN 978-1-890772-83-3 (trade paper : alk. paper)
1. Doulas--Juvenile literature. 2. Natural childbirth--Coaching--Juvenile literature. I. Mithuna, R. Michael, ill. II. Title.
 RG661.H52 2008
 618.4'5--dc22

                    2008013942

HOHM PRESS
P.O. Box 2501
Prescott, AZ 86302
800-381-2700
www.hohmpress.com

This book was printed in China.
Cover Illustration: R. Michael Mithuna

PREFACE

A doula is an experienced helper who provides continuous emotional support and direct assistance to an expecting mother and her family – before, during and after birth. Today, more and more families are turning to a doula to help them through this important rite of passage – the birth of a child.

A doula is not a nurse or a midwife; she does not do anything "medical." She is there to "mother the mother." Each doula is unique, just as each woman giving birth is unique, but all doulas should be nurturing, patient, and have a basic knowledge about and trust in the natural process of birth.

Young children are always very curious about everything that happens to mom or dad, and especially when a new baby is on the way. For many women, a doula becomes a very special person at this time. She may visit their home before or after mom's pregnancy, and children will certainly want to know who this person is.

With simple words and watercolor paintings, *Being Born: The Doula's Role* explains to the young child what a doula is, what she does, and why her role is important when mother is having a baby.

If you are pregnant and don't already have a doula, I hope this book will encourage you to invite one into your life at this special time (see: www.DONA.org). And I hope that you will read this book to your children again and again, talk with them, and answer their questions.

Every day, all over the world,
babies are being born.

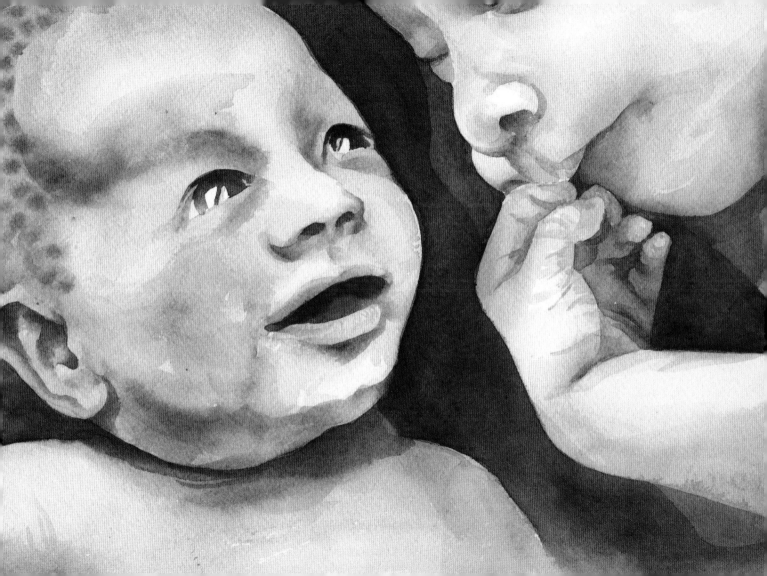

Some are born in grass huts,
some in tall brick buildings.
Some are born in stone houses,
some in houses made of wood.

Some babies are born on the floor, some on beds, and some babies are even born underwater.

Almost all babies are born into the waiting hands of doctors or midwives, fathers or nurses, mothers or grandmothers, sisters or friends.

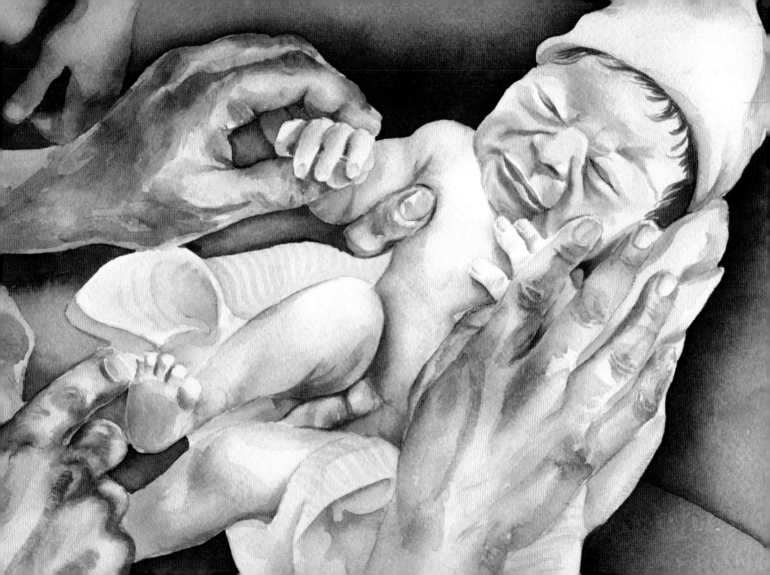

There is a special person who helps a family when they are going to have a baby.

She is called a doula.

A doula might be a sister or a grandmother, or an aunt or a friend.

Some doulas are paid.
Some doulas are volunteers.

It is important for the doula to know what mother likes and dislikes. She finds this out by meeting with the family a few times before their baby is born.

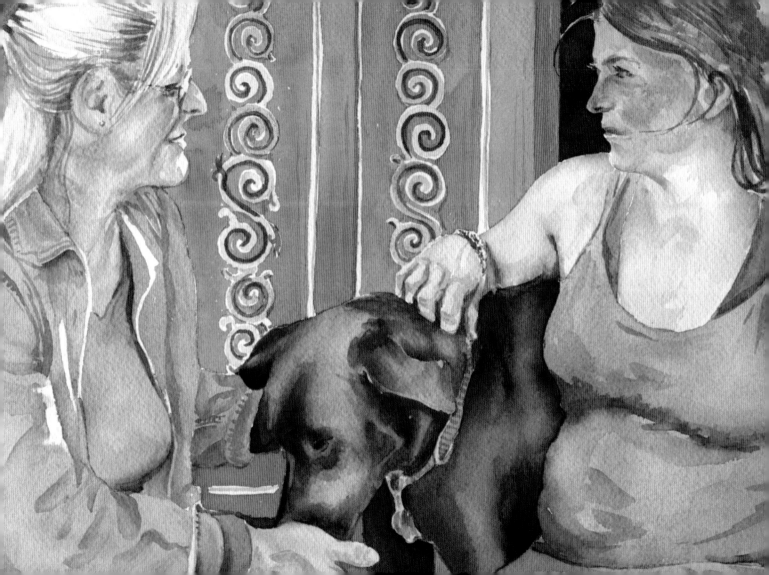

Sometimes the doula helps the family before the baby is born.
She does chores, or cooks, or cares for small children so that mother can get extra rest.

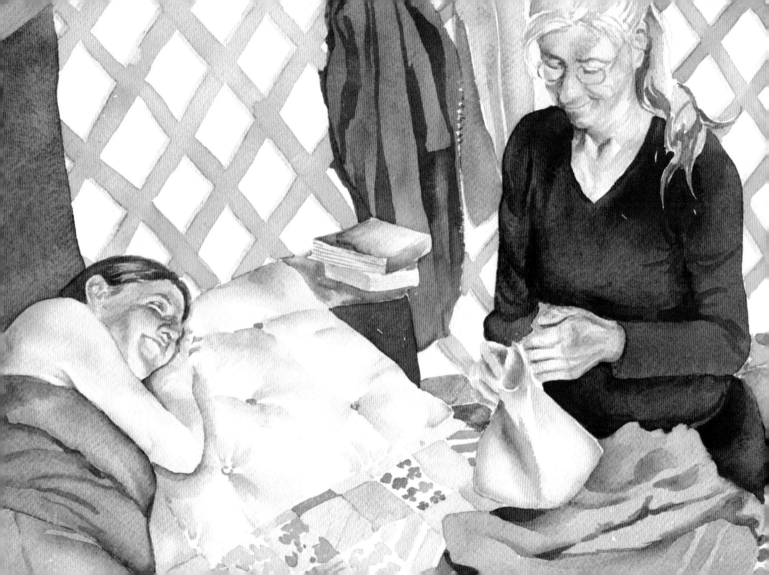

When mother feels her body begin the work of birthing, she calls the doula. Sometimes the doula is called early and sometimes later.

Mother may give birth at home or in a hospital, and the doula will be with her. Once the doula comes, she doesn't leave mother until after the baby is born.

What does the doula do?

She holds mother's hand, wipes her face, gives her water, helps her shower, presses on her back, encourages her, sings to her, rocks with her, and never lets mother forget that she can birth her baby.

After babies are born, they usually want to nurse. Sometimes mother is tired from the hard work she has done. The doula can help guide the baby to mother's breast.

When mother and baby are comfortable, the doula says "Good-bye, and thank you for letting me be at this birth."

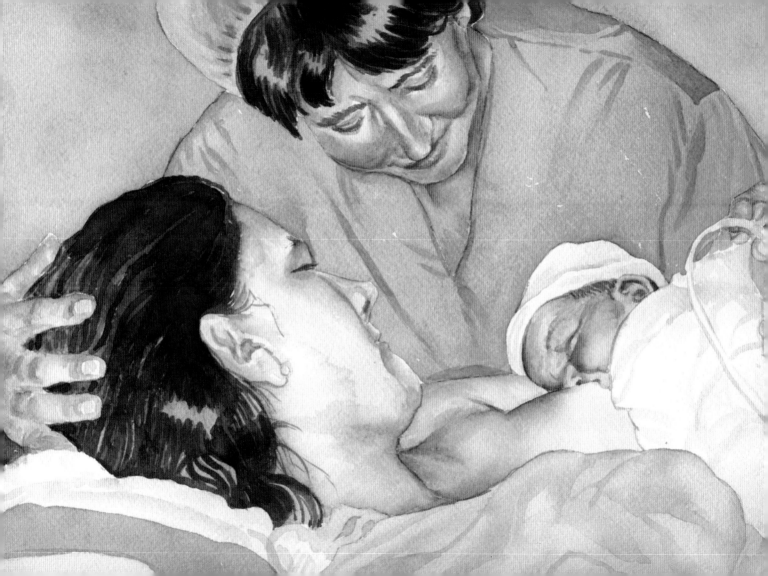

The doula usually visits the family after the baby is born. She shares her story of the birth and any pictures she may have taken.

She answers questions about new babies and nursing. She might even do a load of laundry.

A doula is a very special person. Every woman should have a doula, or someone like her, when she has a baby.

OTHER FAMILY HEALTH TITLES FROM HOHM PRESS

We Like To Nurse
by Chia Martin
Illustrations by Shukyo Rainey
Captivating illustrations present mother animals nursing their young, and honors the mother-child bond created by nursing. (Ages: Infants and up)
ISBN: 978-1-934252-45-4, paper, 32 pages, $9.95
Spanish Language Version: *Nos Gusta Amamanatar*
ISBN: 978-1-890772-41-3

Breastfeeding: Your Priceless Gift To Your Baby and Yourself
by Regina Sara Ryan and Deborah Auletta, R.N., C.L.E.
This inspiring book pleads the case for breastfeeding as the healthiest option for both baby and mom.
ISBN: 978-1-890772-48-2, paper, 64 pages, $9.95
Spanish Language Version: *Amamantar*
ISBN: 978-1-890772-57-4

We Like To Move: Exercise Is Fun
by Elyse April
Illustrations by Diane Iverson
This vividly-colored picture book encourages exercise as a prescription against obesity and diabetes in young children. (Ages: Infants-6)
ISBN: 978-1-890772-60-4, paper, 32 pages, $9.95
Spanish Language Version: *Nos Gusta Movernos: El Ejercicio Es Divertido* ISBN: 978-1-890772-65-9

We Like To Eat Well
by Elyse April
Illustrations by Lewis Agrell
This book celebrates healthy food, and encourages young children and their caregivers to eat well, and with greater awareness. (Ages: Infants-6)
ISBN: 978-1-890772-69-7, paper, 32 pages, $9.95
Spanish Language Version: *Nos Gusta Comer Bien*
ISBN: 978-1-890772-78-9

TO ORDER: *800-381-2700, or visit our website, www.hohmpress.com *Special discounts for bulk orders.*